GLASGOW'S GREATEST EXHIBITION

RECREATING THE 1938 EMPIRE EXHIBITION

EDITED BY IAN JOHNSTON

ACKNOWLEDGEMENTS

The illustrations are largely drawn from
the Reverend Allan collection of colour
transparencies with kind permission of the
Allan family and Neil Baxter and images from
the research work and digital models created
by the Digital Design Studio at the Glasgow
School of Art. Black and white photographs
are from the official Empire Exhibition
collection taken by HM Lawson. It is believed
that these images are in the public domain.

Every effort has been made to obtain
copyright clearance on all the images
within this publication – please address any
enquiries to i.Johnston@gsa.ac.uk

First published 2008 by RIAS, Edinburgh
Copyright; the contributors, Ian Johnston, RIAS
All rights reserved.
ISBN 978-1-873190-59-3
Designed by James Richardson.
A catalogue record for this book is available
from The British Library.

DIGItaL
DesIGn StudIO
THE GLaSGOW
SCHOOL of ARt

House for an Art Lover

Arts & Humanities
Research Council

RIAS
The Royal Incorporation
of Architects in Scotland

FOREWORD

This collection of short essays marks the
completion of the project to recreate the 1938
Empire Exhibition in digital 3D. The project
took the view that the architectural form of the
Exhibition needed to be rehabilitated using state
of the art visualisation technology while the
Exhibition was still within living memory.
Coupled to that was the need to contextualise the
digital output by recording first hand accounts of
the Exhibition given by those who were there.
This booklet concentrates on the original
Exhibition, its influences and the production of
the 3D digital model.

The five essays are intended to introduce
the project and provide a brief overview of
the original event, its influences as well as the
production of the digital recreation.

Neil Baxter provides a general overview of
the reality of the 1938 Exhibition concentrating
on Thomas Tait's role as the principal architect.
Ian Johnston discusses the approach to the
project and how the paucity of primary source
materials was overcome. James Cosgrove reviews
some from the many artworks displayed at the
Exhibition in the context of the buildings they

were housed in while David J Leslie looks at the subsequent careers of some of the architects involved in the Exhibition and touches on its architectural legacy. Finally, Douglas Pritchard gives a short account of the technology involved in making the 3D model.

Although the project succeeded in recreating a very substantial amount of the built Exhibition, building interiors, and the innovative, 12-acre Butlin's Amusement Park in the south east of the Exhibition, remain to be covered.

The results of the work carried out during the course of this project, together with materials gathered from a variety of sources including donations by the public can be accessed at the House for an Art Lover, Bellahouston Park, Glasgow.

The project acknowledges the generous support of the Arts and Humanities Research Council and the House for an Art Lover in providing the funding to make it possible.

IAN JOHNSTON
Editor
May 2008

CONTENTS

PREFACE
PROFESSOR
ANDY MACMILLAN

In 1938 Glasgow was a bustling, grimy city. Imagine then, the splendid vision of a bright new future world that The Empire Exhibition in Bellahouston Park must have presented to a nine year-old boy.

Glorious, clean cut, multi coloured 'modern' glass buildings along wide, splendidly landscaped, boulevards with fountains shooting up everywhere and water cascading down the hill beneath a tall, futuristic tower thrusting up into the sky. At night the bright glow of the new neon lighting rivalled Glasgow's other source of night-time lighting, the famous Dixon's Blazes foundry. What a vision!

The interiors of the pavilions were also new and exciting. Marvellous displays, buttons to press and new things to discover. There was even a representation of the Victoria Falls, crashing down thunderously in a welter of spray. What an experience for a youngster and the citizens of the dirty old town. Was this perhaps when I subconsciously decided to become an architect?

The War intervened and I went on to secondary school. When the war ended in 1945, I started an architectural apprenticeship in Glasgow Housing Department, becoming involved, paradoxically, in an exhibition of the brave new world post-war houses 'Fit For Heroes' that were being proposed. A flashback to that brilliant exhibition.

An even closer connection came about when I went to work for Jack Coia, one of Glasgow's leading architects who had been a member of the architectural team which had designed the Exhibition.

Jack had designed the Palace of Engineering North and the Roman Catholic Church Pavilion as well as the Exhibition's very modern street furniture. He liked to talk about working with Tommy Tait, the chief Architect of the Exhibition.

These connections, I am sure, were among the reasons why I recently found myself on the panel of historians, architects and artists who were working on a project to recreate the 1938 Exhibition digitally. Our role was to help the 3D modellers ensure that the reconstruction was as accurate as possible.

Why seek to recreate the 1938 Exhibition and what lay behind this project? The Exhibition had been the biggest of its kind in pre-war Britain, the epitome of 1930s architecture of the time, demonstrating the talent of Scottish architects – a showcase for the world.

The House for an Art Lover is not only a visitor centre in Bellahouston Park where the Exhibition was sited, but houses Glasgow School of Art's Digital Design Studio, a centre for 3D visualisation, interaction and masters education. The Digital Design Studio was funded to conduct this project into the Exhibition and produce a 3D model of it for scholars and the public to enjoy. It was felt that recreating the exhibition would not only be a challenging test of skill, an exercise at the cutting edge, but that it could also assess what impact it had made on architecture and perhaps even on the country, at the time, as well as looking at its legacy.

In the making of the project, a comprehensive archive of artefacts was created including recorded interviews with people who had visited. A bit of living social history then, as well as photographs, plans, films, books, souvenirs and newspaper articles.

Both the 3D reconstruction and the archive created by the project form an important educational resource which this small book augments. It is hoped that this will encourage further research.

As the project began to present the external forms of the Exhibition, it became clear that some of the buildings are astonishingly 'modern' even today. Much work remains to be done however, and it is hoped that it will be possible to address the interiors of some of the more outstanding pavilions as well as explore the public art so clearly visible in the photographic records; graphics, sculpture, murals, banners, flags and all the exciting artworks which so animated this vision of the brave new world I saw as a nine year old child.

So I commend the visitor to the House for an Art Lover , to enjoy and to learn. I highly commend the rigour of the 3D modelling team with whom I had the pleasure of working , and would add a special word of praise for Ian Johnston who led the Project.

A.MACMILLAN
May 2008

LEFT. A dramatic simulation of the Victoria Falls in the Southern Rhodesia and East Africa Pavilion. ABOVE. A striking early artist's rendering by Hugh Watt of the Tower of Empire.

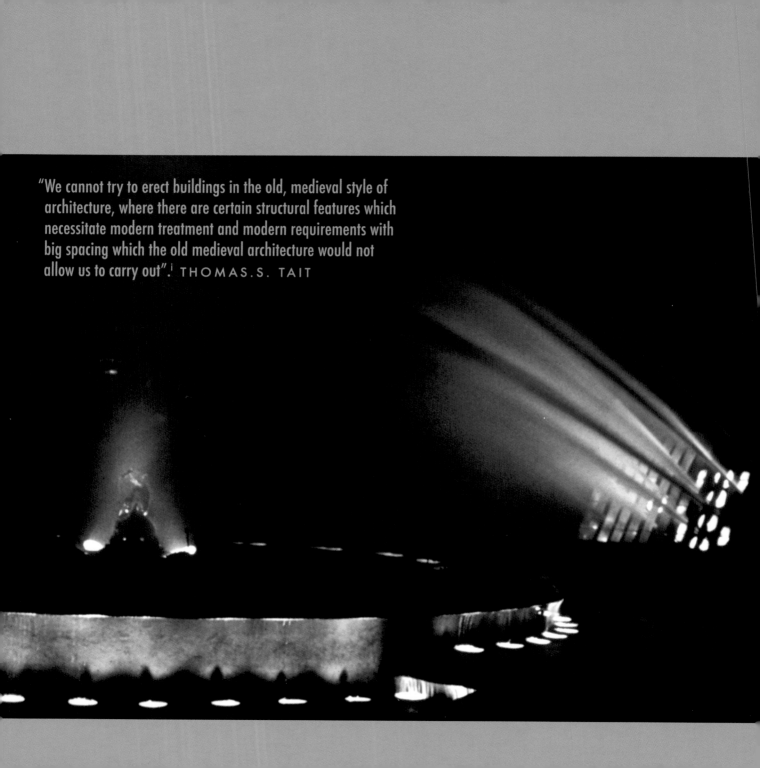

"We cannot try to erect buildings in the old, medieval style of architecture, where there are certain structural features which necessitate modern treatment and modern requirements with big spacing which the old medieval architecture would not allow us to carry out".[i] THOMAS.S. TAIT

1 THOMAS S. TAIT AND THE 1938 EMPIRE EXHIBITION

NEIL BAXTER, ARCHITECTURAL HISTORIAN
THE ROYAL INCORPORATION OF ARCHITECTS IN SCOTLAND

The Empire Exhibition of 1938, Glasgow's fourth major exhibition, was the most concentrated and comprehensive display of the 'New Architecture' seen anywhere in Britain before the 1939-45 war. From the outset the organisers were ambitious. The chosen site, Bellahouston Park, at around 175 acres was sufficient area for the largest exhibition held anywhere since the 1924 British Empire Exhibition held at Wembley. The 1938 Exhibition's palaces and pavilions combined to produce the nearest thing to a townscape of modern buildings in the inter-war period.

The choice of architect-in-chief presented few problems. The official line was that a competition, although desirable, was precluded by the lack of time. The organisation committee's unanimous choice for the job was Thomas S. Tait of the London firm of Sir John Burnet, Tait and Lorne.

Tait, born in Paisley and educated in Glasgow, had recently completed the prestigious government commission for St. Andrew's House on Edinburgh's Calton Hill. As architect-in-chief, Tait was required to plan an elaborate layout, to organise the design and supervise the construction of numerous palaces and pavilions. The size of the scheme demanded the employment of several assistants to each of whom was allocated the design of a particular building, or buildings. These architects were selected from what Tait described as the 'younger school of Scottish Architects'.[ii]

Tait had to create buildings which were inexpensive, could be rapidly and easily constructed and despite the number of architects involved, would combine to form a homogeneous whole.

The site, Bellahouston Park, had the advantage of being bounded on two sides by major roads. Vehicular access was therefore straight forward and Tait did not have to plan around existing roads or other obstacles. However, the heavily wooded central hill restricted the area upon which the principal buildings could be erected to the level ground on the north, south and west of the site.

The floodlit water display from the parabolic jet system installed in The Lake. The extensive water features at the Exhibition were developed by Crouch & Hogg, Consulting Engineers.

BELLAHOUSTON PARK 1937

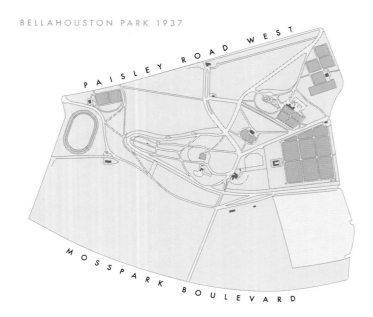

BELLAHOUSTON PARK 1938

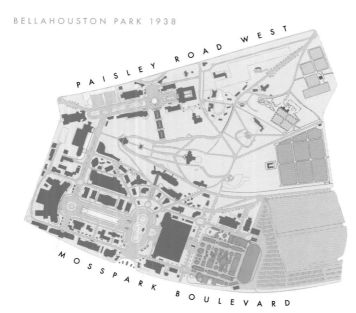

The Exhibition's dual role, to illustrate the unity of the British Empire and demonstrate the United Kingdom's resources and progress, necessitated three main types of building. Tait had to group together, in discrete areas, the pavilions of the dominions and colonies, buildings representing the life and culture of the British Isles and those buildings which demonstrated British achievement in engineering and manufacturing.

Tait revelled in his planning task and the thrill of being able to say, "Let there be an avenue here and here and here".[iii]

The ground plan, presented to the organisation committee early in 1937, detailed an arrangement of buildings around three main axes. The largest structures, the Palace of Industries West and the Palace of Engineering, lay on the expanse to the south of the central hill. These were positioned at either end of an avenue which was flanked by dominion and colonial pavilions. To separate the large industrial pavilions from those representing the nations of the Empire, Tait used large, elaborately planted flower beds. The rows of dominion and colonial pavilions were separated by a long, narrow lake. Thus two distinct avenues were formed.

To the west of the hill, and at right angles to the dominions and colonial avenue, ran the avenue upon which the British Government Pavilion was to be built. This avenue was later

The map at top shows the 175-acre Bellahouston Park as it was in 1937, prior to work commencing on the Exhibition. The map below shows Tait's masterplan where 3 major avenues were wrapped around the whaleback ridge that dominated the park. The area in red shows the extent of Butlin's amusement park in the south-east corner.

TOP LEFT. The North Cascade at night showing the use of coloured lights in the water display. LEFT. The dynamic Pavilion for the Scottish Motor Transport Co. complete with bus. BOTTOM LEFT. The careful depiction of a highland village, An Clachan, designed by Dr Colin Sinclair. ABOVE. The National Fitness Pavilion drawing a large audience to watch a display in progress. Then as now, the pursuit of physical fitness was in vogue.

named Kingsway. On the north side of the hill between the Palace of Arts and the Concert Hall was an avenue flanked by the two Scottish Pavilions. Although most of the important structures were built upon the three axes described, the potential of the hill as a site for imposing structures was noted as early as November 1936. In February 1937, along with his layout plan, Tait presented sketches for an impressive observation tower to be built on the summit of the hill. Two massive stairways on a direct line with the main entrances would provide easy access to this dramatic centrepiece of the exhibition.

The area to the east of the park was not to be used as part of the exhibition proper, but would accommodate the more frivolous features of the enterprise. It was planned to build an amusement park along with restaurant and dance hall in the south-eastern corner, and a highland village, following in the tradition of 'Clachans' at Glasgow exhibitions, in the north-eastern area.

The Extraordinary demands imposed by the exhibition forced Tait to diverge from his normally conservative methods. By adopting a design system based on standard components Tait ensured that the buildings, designed by different architects, would blend in their modernity and scale. Materials, component sizes, colours and the designs of smaller buildings were all standardised. As the Exhibition's buildings were to be constructed on both steel and timber frames, the cladding had to be suitable for both. Tait decided that asbestos-cement sheeting, light, weather resistant and easily painted, best suited his purpose.

The standard cladding sheets dictated the proportions of each structure. Internal frames, windows and entrance openings were all calculated as sub-divisions or multiples of the 'unit', similarly this rectangular unit became the basis of the grid, dictating both elevation and plan of each building. The unit size was sufficiently large to exclude trivial or over-elaborate detail and a plethora of different designs were given common scale. Tait's adoption of standard parts ensured that his Exhibition had order and unity.

Beyond his layout and stipulations regarding materials, Tait directly supervised the design of

View of the south-west corner seen from the Tower of Empire showing the Canadian Pavilion at centre and the Industries Pavilions, top right, with Mosspark Boulevard behind.

something over half of the Exhibition's structures. Control of the British Government Pavilion and those of the dominions and colonies had been delegated elsewhere early in the planning stage. The lack of direct input from Tait may account for the clumsy combination of heavy massing with minimal glazing in several of the latter.

Tait's influence upon the Exhibition's individual designs was two-fold, arising from the design principles he dictated and from his own eclectic approach. Throughout his career Tait assimilated styles or stylistic details and adjusted them to suit the desires of his client and restrictions of site and budget. Nowhere is this talent more overtly expressed than in the 1938 Empire Exhibition. Although Tait's degree of control over those structures for which he shares the credit is undocumented, in several instances clear precedents can be traced in his previous work and experience.

In obedience to Tait's insistence on the use of contemporary methods of construction and up to date materials his assistants were limited to a range of essentially 'modern' variations.

A crucial precedent for Tait's use of standard parts was Mendelsohn and Chermayeff's De la Warr Pavilion, Bexhill (1935). Tait was the sole judge of the Bexhill competition. The lessons taught by the winning design had a considerable effect upon his Exhibition scheme. The seaside pavilion's role as a general precedent, through its structural system, affected virtually every aspect of the 1938 Exhibition's design. However the most overt visual connection is with one of the Exhibition's most acclaimed structures: the Garden Club.

The Club's long hillside site dictated the emphasis upon its front elevation. Acknowledging the primary importance of this aspect, Tait working with the young Edinburgh architect, T.W. Marwick, produced a sweeping boundary wall in a dramatic double curve. This curve was repeated in the stepped levels of the raised ground and first floors.

A humourously literal sign located by the Royal Reception Rooms at the eastern end of Scottish Avenue.

LEFT. Early rendering of the Garden Club. BELOW LEFT. The restaurant in the Garden Club with its strikingly modern layout.

The Garden Club was composed in three sections reading, from left to right: rotunda (a circular arrangement of sales kiosks), colonnade (open to give access to the hill behind), and club/restaurant (designed to serve as an exclusive meeting place). The rear of the building, relatively dark and backing onto the hill, was utilised for the services necessary to cater for large numbers of people. Purely functional, these offices do not share the curving forms of the front elevation. In the Exhibition as a whole, curved or undulating lines were preferred for aesthetic effect.

While the Bexhill scheme, with its similarly long front elevation and protruding oval stairwell, influenced Tait's approach to the Garden Club, the latter building is neither as bare nor as sharply defined as its predecessor. Admittedly, the Exhibition demanded bold and bright structures; but the avoidance of the De la Warr Pavilion's grave geometry in the Garden Club also demonstrates the natural reticence of its controlling designer.

It seems likely that, while Tait determined the general form and massing of the Garden Club, Marwick was responsible for its detailed design, execution, fine detailing and decoration. The Garden Club drew much favourable critical comment.

Marwick designed two other structures in the Exhibition: a small pavilion in the eastern area of the site, and the Atlantic Restaurant. The latter, a piece of architectural whimsy on the brow of Bellahouston Hill, might be considered the ultimate realization of the nautical theme in British 'Moderne' architecture. A straight imitation of a ship's prow, rather than any adaptation of 'motifs', it lacks the inspiration which guided the design of the Garden Club.

However for obvious reasons the Tower became the public favourite. Much interest focused on technical details: at around 300 feet this was the tallest enclosed structure yet built in Britain. Its foundation block provided a similarly awe inspiring statistic: 3,500 tons of concrete (still inside Bellahouston Hill).

The emphasised stepping of oblong masses in Tait's Tower relates the structure to the architect's previous forays in the style of the Dutch master W.M. Dudok. Tait employed a similar conjunction of oblong blocks, imitative of the water tower of Dudok's Hilversum Town Hall (1931), in the entrance pillars to his Paisley Infectious Diseases Hospital and in the pylons flanking the entrance of St. Andrew's House. In the Tower the motif is, as J.H. Gould put it, 'in excelsis', the conjunction exaggerated on a massive scale. This layered effect also reduced the direct wind loading – a crucial consideration for such an exposed structure.

The deployment of the Tower's observation balconies was also derivative. Gropius and Meyer had employed layered cantilevered balconies in their submission for the Chicago Tribune Tower Competition (1922). It is more likely however that Tait knew the device from his visit to the Paris 1925 (Art-Deco) Exhibition where it appeared, greatly scaled down, in the clock-tower of Rob Mallet-Steven's tourism pavilion.

Designed to a higher specification than the Exhibition's other structures, the Tower was built in the same way with its riveted metal frame clad in prepared sheets. Perhaps a somewhat overblown pastiche, certainly ambitious for a lift shaft, the Tower's popularity testifies to its success as a spectacular focus for the exhibition.

Numerous parallels with this pivotal design appeared in the Exhibition in many free-standing fins and in other buildings which featured towers. Among the latter were the two 'mirror image' pavilions which flanked the Scottish Avenue. Designed by Tait and the young, Edinburgh educated architect, Basil Spence, the Scottish Pavilions were among the Exhibition's most prestigious features.

Basil Spence's twin Scottish Pavilions viewed from the North Cascade with the Campsie Fells in the distance.

The towers on the Scottish Pavilions reduce the scale and modify the design of the structure which overlooked them from Bellahouston Hill. Combining only two vertical 'members', the simpler and smaller of which projects forward and wraps around the other, they also multiply the horizontal striation pattern originated in the Tower's balconies.

The real advance of the Scottish Pavilion design, which anticipated and possibly influenced post-war developments, arose from its adaptation of Dudok. By constructing interpenetrating blocky masses in clad-frame, rather than brick, Tait and Spence produced a work in a style which would become commonplace in the 1950s. Here the Dudok influence is apparent in massing rather than articulation, the articulation arising directly from the frame. The opening of the structure in the glazing of the facade was much praised in contemporary accounts.

A highly worked sketch by Spence, published early in 1937, suggests that his was the predominant influence on the Scottish Pavilion design. This is consistent with his considerable design experience if not his relative youth.

The decoration of the Scottish Pavilions seems applied as an afterthought rather than an integral part of the design. In Spence's small pavilion for ICI however, decoration and design are completely integrated. This pavilion was fancifully Moderne in design. It consisted of a rotunda and three pylons adorned with symbolic motifs. The pylons were linked by a series of metal bars behind which there played a fountain. In common with much of the rest of the Exhibition, this pavilion was fitted with dramatic lighting, adding to the spectacle of the Exhibition by night.

The only building comparable in 'functional' aesthetic effect to Spence's Scottish Pavilions was Jack Coia's Palace of Industry North. Although a late inclusion necessitated by the over-subscription of the main Palace of Industries, this building was constructed with remarkable speed in the weeks leading up to the Exhibition. This huge, extensively glazed structure resembles a row of aircraft hangars joined on their longest edge. The dramatic entrance from Kingsway (on the corner) again finds its roots in Bexhill.

Coia's other building, the Roman Catholic Pavilion, demonstrates the craft roots of his design technique. While the materials of its construction

BELOW. A Lister auto-truck speeding past the Scottish Daily Express Creche. There were 50 of these trucks covering five different routes over the 10 miles of Exhibition roads. BOTTOM. The cantilevered canopy of the South Bandstand designed by Thomas Tait complete with mural. OPPOSITE. Advertising hoardings on the structure that screened the Exhibition from the bowling greens at Paisley Road West.

were new and the design remarkably unembellished, this structure retains the traditional effect of Coia's earlier Glasgow work for the Roman Catholic Church.

Just how the public reacted to this unprecedented onslaught of modernism is difficult to gauge. A popular vote selected the Dutch Colonial style, South African Pavilion, the only building in the Exhibition to deviate entirely from Tait's guidance, as the public's favourite. However Tait's Tower itself was and remains the most talked about structure in the show, indeed arguably in Glasgow's history.

The attendance at the Exhibition was poorer than expected (although still over 12.5 million) and the event lost money, no doubt more a response to the stormy weather of the summer of 1938 than a reaction to the Exhibition's architecture. In any case the Exhibition was an extravagant fantasy playground, its transience augmenting this effect, (the Exhibition opened on the 3rd of May and ran for six months).

The architecture of the 1938 Empire Exhibition was exciting and experimental. The Exhibition's modernism was, however, a product of the vagaries of time and finance, despite Tait's insistence that he was overthrowing the 'old medieval style'. Appreciating the problems of such a project Tait devised a system which acknowledged the suitability of pre-fabricated design to the scheme. In the exhibition's better buildings this functional priority was reconciled with the secondary, but vital, aesthetic aspect.

The Exhibition was a creative triumph, sparkling, original and ready on time (the Wembley Exhibition of 1924 and the Paris Exposition International of 1937 were not). Tait responded with vigour to his extraordinary organisational task. In the process he created a spectacle of monumental proportions and extraordinary brilliancy which vividly endures in memory.

This article is adapted and updated from the piece of the same title which appeared in the The Thirties Society Journal, 1984.

i   Glasgow Herald, 26.2.37, p7.
ii Glasgow Herald, 6.10.36, p11.
iii T.S. Tait 'Planning The Empire Exhibition', SMT and Scottish Country Life, May 1938, p.88.

2 RECREATING THE 1938 BRITISH EMPIRE EXHIBITION

IAN JOHNSTON, EMPIRE PROJECT LEADER,
THE DIGITAL DESIGN STUDIO, GLASGOW SCHOOL OF ART

In 2005 a successful bid to fund research into the 1938 Empire Exhibition with the aim of constructing detailed 3D digital models of the Exhibition was submitted to the Arts & Humanities Research Council. The bid was largely based around the argument that the legacy of this significant Exhibition had been extinguished by the start of World War Two in September 1939, less than one year after the Exhibition ended. Thus, the argument went, there had been little reflection or debate about the 1938 architectural forms that would become ubiquitous in the 1950s and 60s. Nevertheless, the Exhibition was within living memory and while much of the project was concentrated on the technical process of recreating its physicality, interviews were conducted with people who had visited in 1938 to ensure that the virtual model could be contextualised with descriptions and recollections from those who were there.

While the technical method involved in creating 3D models was generally straightforward, the real issue concerned the relatively small amount of detailed architectural information that had survived since 1938. Although a number of floor plans and elevation drawings found in architectural journals were used, the 3D modelling team assembled for this project relied mainly on an extensive collection of still photography and movie footage. Crucially, it was recognised that 3D visualisation software allows inaccuracies and embellishments to be passed off as fact. To preserve the academic rigour of the modelling process and the integrity of the original building designs, a panel of architects, designers and historians was also assembled and placed in the modelling loop to assess each building and its virtual representation as work progressed. All decisions, whether issues of scale or architectural detail, were based on drawings or photographs or informed by this panel. These decisions were recorded and attached to the model for future reference. Before describing how the Exhibition was recreated, researchers and modellers at the Digital Design Studio considered the historical context from which the new, digital Exhibition would be framed.

An official photograph of the British Railways Pavilion designed by Joseph Emberton. This reference to British Railways predated the formation of the nationalised company in 1948 and showcased the four mainline railway companies then operating in the UK.

BACKGROUND – 1938 EMPIRE EXHIBITION

Buildings that no longer exist pose a serious problem in attempting to reconstruct them accurately in the form of 3D digital models. Setting aside the argument that the every day environment and cultural atmosphere that buildings exist within is an important element in their historical reconstruction, providing a simple but accurate record of their physicality alone is demanding enough.

In the case of buildings that were intended from the outset to be of a temporary nature additional problems exist. The 1938 Empire Exhibition was conceived in 1936 as a means of addressing several issues. Such an Exhibition, extolling the virtues of the Empire was considered to be 'overdue' as the last one, held at Wembley, was in 1924. Unfavourable economic circumstances throughout the 1920s and early 30s, and the hardship endured across Britain as a result, had militated against such a display of imperial pomp. Glasgow, the second largest city in Britain, and the centre of a vast industrial empire in its own right, was emerging from the depression as production and employment began to rise against a background of rearmament. It seemed an opportune time to place economic recovery, together with Britain's previously impressive industrial track record, in the form of a major event. Thus the 1938 Empire Exhibition was brought into existence as a well funded and elaborately detailed world event at which no expense would be spared.

ABOVE. The Glasgow Pavilion designed by Glasgow's Office of Public Works. OPPOSITE. This drawing is one of very few to survive from 1938. *Courtesy of Archives and Special Collections, Mitchell Library, Glasgow.*

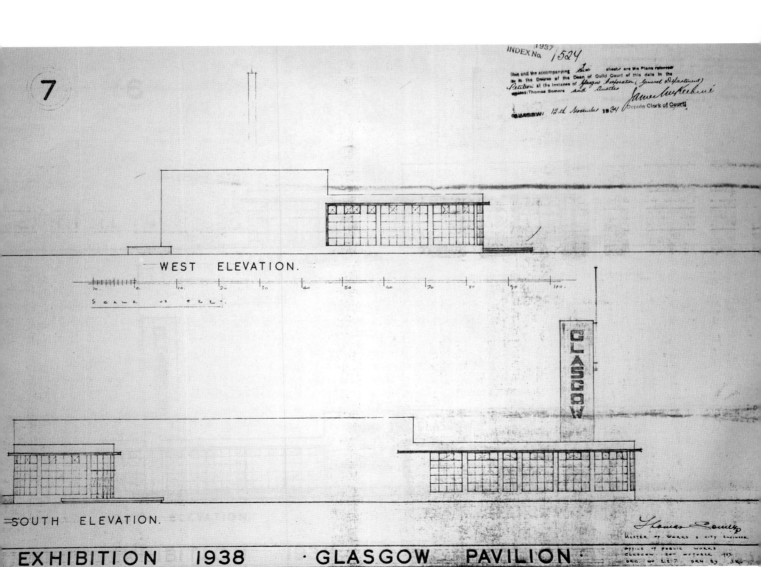

WEST ELEVATION.

SOUTH ELEVATION.

EXHIBITION 1938 · GLASGOW PAVILION ·

The large murals by C.L.Davidson fronting the entrance to the Palace of Engineering had to be recreated as two 2D images and applied to the 3D model. The subject matter was very pertinent to the industries of Clydeside. At top is HMS Hood, largest warship in the world while the bottom image shows the Cunarder RMS Queen Mary. Both ships were built by John Brown at Clydebank.

The site chosen to house the Exhibition was the 175-acre Bellahouston Park to the south and west of Glasgow city centre. The topography of this site was at once complex but rich in possibility. Dominated by a hill approximately in the middle of the park, architect Thomas Tait chose to wrap three main avenues and associated buildings around the base of the hill while surmounting it with a 100-metre tower, The Tower of Empire. Ninety significant buildings were constructed on site plus many minor ones. Water, in the form of fountains and lakes, was used to spectacular effect as was lighting which made extensive use of neon for the first time in the UK. Broad avenues and many subsidiary roadways were

laid out, fitted with well-designed street furniture ranging from impressive lighting standards to swivel topped, pressed-steel, waste bins. The buildings were mostly of temporary construction, timber framed, with asbestos sheet and plywood panels. A few, such as The Tower of Empire and the Palace of Engineering were steel framed and sheet metal clad. Only one building was designed to be retained on site after the Exhibition closed, The Palace of Art.

The Exhibition was opened by the King and Queen in May 1938. It closed on the last day of October having attracted an audience of nearly 13 million people. The buildings were sold off and dismantled quickly thereafter as always intended although a few that had not yet been demolished found a use on site during the early years of World War Two.

The principal dilemma presented by the award of funding however was to ensure that in building digital models where little primary information existed, invention and embellishment were ruled out. To safeguard the integrity of the project both academically and architecturally, an appropriate working methodology evolved.

VIRTUAL RECONSTRUCTION METHODOLOGY

Every significant building erected in the UK is subject to a bureaucratic process centred around planning application and building control compliance. Despite its temporary nature, formal architectural procedures were followed in building the 1938 Exhibition with drawings prepared for visualisation, planning and construction purposes. However, in the case of the many buildings erected for the Empire Exhibition, only twelve sets of architectural drawings were found during the research phase of this project. As architects' drawings must be considered as the primary source of accurate information where the buildings no longer exist, this was a major setback.

The dearth of primary source material was partly because there was little need to preserve drawings for buildings that were no longer there. Further drawings had been lost through accidents, floods, fires and the other calamities that befall architects offices and archived collections. Examination of the surviving architects' drawings, prepared for Dean of Guild submission, revealed a further complication – many of the drawings show buildings that differ in detail from the 'as built' structures evident in photographs and cine film.

Recourse was therefore made to secondary sources, principal of which were the drawings reproduced in architectural journals at the time, such as Architectural Review. Here, small-scale drawings derived from full-scale architectural drawings had been prepared for reproduction.

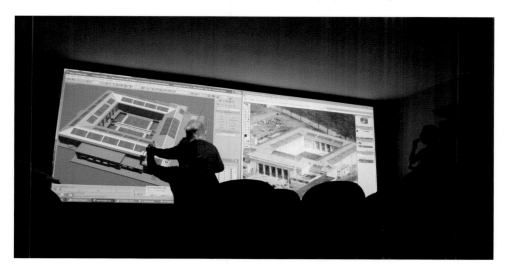

Professor Andy MacMillan reviewing the 3D model of the Palace of Art during the construction phase. A photograph of the actual building is projected to the right of the 3D model for easy reference. Iwan Peverett, 3D modeller, is watching with interest from the right.

While possibly dimensionally accurate, they did not show details that would make the reconstructed models more interesting. Would they reflect modifications or in situ adaptations made necessary during construction? Time would tell. Either way, the integrity of drawings from this source was questionable.

The other source of information was found in the numerous photographs and movies made at the time. One very good set of 35mm colour transparencies existed, the collection of photographs taken by the Reverend Allan, plus an extensive set of official black and white photographs by Lawson, that covered much of the Exhibition. However, the natural inclination of photographers to take the most glamorous shots meant that the photographs rarely covered rear and side elevations. These elevations were often evident only incidentally in shots of other buildings. Other publications such as The London Illustrated News or The Engineer published at the time were useful in providing general information and details such as letterforms and other interesting incidentals.

ABOVE. A black and white photograph showing the Atlantic Restaurant and the southern plain of Bellahouston Park extending to Mosspark Boulevard. LEFT. The 3D model of the same view.

Cine film shot at the time, some in colour, was made available by the Scottish Film Archive while other films were contributed by members of the public in response to good newspaper coverage of the project. This coverage proved to be invaluable, prompting many members of the pubic to donate memorabilia purchased at the time.

Although the consulting engineers attached to the project in 1938, Crouch & Hogg, now Halcrow, were approached, they had not retained any relevant information. However, a member of the public submitted a large-scale OS based ground plan, stamped by Thomas Tait's office, showing the Exhibition as it was six months before completion. Although inaccurate in parts, it was sufficiently complete to permit a more accurate version to be prepared using photographs and the simple ground plan published in the Exhibition Handbook.

This then was the sum total of the graphic information available from which to recreate the 1938 Empire Exhibition in 3D - hundreds of monochrome and colour stills, movie footage, a handful of architectural drawings and small-scale plans published in journals.

ABOVE. The 3D model of the Peace Pavilion showing interesting lighting effects where the shadows from the trees have been reflected onto the building. The wording on the signs at either side of the steps was carefully recreated. BELOW. The black and white photograph taken prior to the addition of the signs.

THE PANEL

Given the lack of primary research materials such as architectural drawings, the Panel assumed a more immediate importance to the process of recreating the Exhibition than originally intended. The panel comprised two architects, David J Leslie and Andy MacMillan, a historian, Neil Baxter and a designer, James Cosgrove, who were well versed in the Exhibition. Moreover, one of the Panel, Emeritus Professor Andy MacMillan, formerly head of the Mackintosh School of Architecture, had worked with one of the Exhibition's architects, Jack Coia, and felt as close to the mindset of the original architects as was possible nearly seventy years later.

The panel reviewed every Exhibition building under construction by the 3D modelling team requesting updates, deletions or corrections to ensure that models were as close to the visual reference material and 'mindset'

as possible and that treatments given to hidden elevations were either sympathetically worked or not worked at all. Each model was subjected to this process repeatedly if necessary until it was signed off by the Panel.

It was agreed that where no information was available nothing would be invented beyond continuing what was obvious in the form of cladding or treatment of copes, lintels etc. To make this very clear to subsequent researchers, it was agreed that notes would accompany each model describing the reference material used to create it and pointing to areas where no information was available.

THE MODELLING SOFTWARE

Presently, 3D modelling software such as that used to create the buildings of the Exhibition has the ability to produce work that looks photo-real. This is at once satisfying to behold but potentially misleading where the source material is incomplete. By its very nature, software is 'absolutist' in its numerical definition of the objects it purports to represent. In presenting such a dimensionally and photographically perfect world, 3D models can easily be mistaken for reality or as an accurate representation of something that no longer exists.

The 3D model of the North Cascade complete with water effects, coloured lights and flower beds. Understandably the Union flag was much in prominence as were the flags of the constituent nations in this instance England and Scotland.

If any sense of academically derived process was to be applied to the Empire Exhibition project, a series of caveats were written into the modelling process. If software applies precise parameters to every element of a 3D model, so too can the assumptions held by modellers be transferred knowingly or unknowingly to the models they build. The modelling of every building was therefore thoroughly documented by the modelling team. They noted how their virtual representations were built and whether or not they were based on existing drawings, photographs or other information.

The output for the project included print-quality images, animations and an extensive website. In addition to the website, all research materials collected during the project as well as the digital resource, has been archived for public consumption at the House for an Art Lover, Glasgow which just happens to be located in Bellahouston Park, the site of the original 1938 Exhibition.

Over the fifteen month duration of this project a highly detailed 3D model of the 1938 Empire Exhibition was created. While a fully accurate reconstruction of any building or structure that no longer exists is impossible to achieve, the procedures utilised in this project provide a basis for a 'qualified' level of accuracy. Digital embellishments within the structures were eliminated and where judgements were made in the absence of fact, notes were attached to the model listing actions and assumptions. With continuing improvements in software capability and the consequent desire to take realism to new levels of user experience, attempts to recreate the past, as there surely will be, must be approached with enthusiasm and caution in equal measure!

An aerial view of the completed model viewed from the south-west.

The United Kingdom Pavilion,
a night-time illustrative sketch
showing reflections in the water.
The crest above the exit was
replaced by a relief of Britania and
a bridge created across the lake

3 TWELVE EMPIRE BUILDINGS
A PERSONAL VIEW
JAMES COSGROVE, ARTIST AND DESIGNER

"A city of light, colour, spaciousness, spectacle and gaiety".
CONTEMPORARY DESCRIPTION OF THE EMPIRE EXHIBITION

THE ATLANTIC RESTAURANT

Probably the most light hearted building in the Exhibition, the Atlantic Restaurant provided a counter-point to the serious business of promoting industrial strength and diverse cultures. Based on the prow of a ship emerging out of the hillside on the west slope of Bellahouston Hill, the building was a cleverly designed and witty 'folly', with tea decks and bridge/balcony built over an access road from which services and goods were delivered. The cocktail bar and restaurant were supervised by waiters dressed like ship's stewards, in keeping with the nautical theme .

Thomas Marwick designed the building in association with the architect-in-chief, Thomas Tait whose Tower of Empire could be reached further up the hill. The Atlantic Restaurant's main deck was built round a commemorative stone unveiled by the King in 1937 prior to the building of the Exhibition. He returned there to lunch with Queen Elizabeth at the opening of the Exhibition on 3 May 1938.

The digital representation of the magnificent Atlantic Restaurant and Tower of Empire lit up at night showing the brilliant lighting effects that characterised the Exhibition.

The curved facade of the restaurant which marked the western extent of the Scottish Avenue.

THE CONCERT HALL AND RESTAURANT

The inverted curve of the front elevation of the Concert Hall Restaurant was raised on steel columns. The form was similar to the Treetops Restaurant at the foot of the Tower of Empire, its elevated position allowing diners unobstructed views along the Scottish Avenue to the Scottish Pavilions and the Palace of Art. It also provided a spacious loggia below for audiences to gather and access the Concert Hall foyer. It was a colourful arrangement with columns in blue and staircase walls washed in brown. The end walls of the restaurant were bright pink.

The internal walls of the Concert Hall featured panels painted by Glasgow artist Hugh Adam Crawford. In the centre of the forecourt was a bronze group, by the sculptor Pilkington Jackson, entitled 'Sea Foam', one figure of which appeared to be pushed forward by spray from the sea.

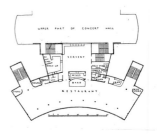

THE PALACE OF ART

A digital view of the Palace of Art which marked the easternmost extent of the Scottish Avenue.

Planned from the outset as the only building to be retained after the Exhibition, as a gallery to house part of the City's collection of art, the Palace of Art was built using permanent materials. Its architect, Launcelot Ross was also responsible for the Exhibition's largest building – the Palace of Engineering.

The building is austerly classical in style with an impressive colonnaded entrance flanked by two rectangular wings.

The internal garden, open to the elements, provided an oasis for contemplation away from the hustle and bustle outside. A sculpture of Pan by Charles Jagger was a prominent piece at the head of a small pool of water.

Exhibitions of paintings within the Palace were grouped in two main collections; a retrospective Scottish section and a modern British collection. Pictures by Raeburn, Ramsay and Wilkie catered for most tastes while the 'Glasgow School' challenged perceptions about modern art. Bold, colourful works by Ferguson, Peploe and Cadell spearheaded 'the modern movement'. British modernism was similarly represented by Walter Sickert, Wilson Steer and Augustus John, leading an impressive range of contemporary artists.

Works by around 250 artists filled the seven galleries, and, unusually for Glasgow, visitors paid sixpence admission charge to be enlightened and entertained by a very impressive gathering of Scottish art within a British context.

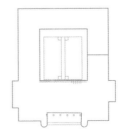

ROMAN CATHOLIC CHURCH PAVILION

Perched on the south slope of Bellahouston Hill, below Tait's Tower, this unusually formed and decorated pavilion combined a Mission Hall, where the work of the Catholic Church across the Empire was exhibited, an open-air oratory and a Hall of Ecclesiastical Art. The focal point of the building, at the end of the open oratory, was the altar-shrine where Mass was celebrated.

Jack Coia, architect behind several innovative Catholic churches before and after this Pavilion, was an avowed collaborator with artists and crafts-people who exploited the use of brick, timber and wrought iron, thereby enabling him to deploy some of the city's best painters, sculptors, stained glass artists and blacksmiths to fashion artworks within and around the building. This can be seen in the ironwork at the entrance to the building and in the large ecclesiastical vignettes which decorate the windowless white exterior.

RIGHT. Painted figures decorate the otherwise austere surface of the building. BELOW. Coia's drawing of the front elevation showing the entrance screen and the elegant campanile.

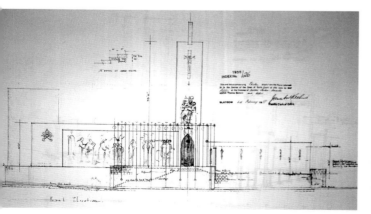

UNITED KINGDOM PAVILION

The United Kingdom Pavilion designed by Herbert J Rowse, was an imposing venue for an educational display of the country's three great industrial assets, coal, iron and steel and shipbuilding. Each was allocated a large self-contained gallery, with a main entrance off an extraordinarily high and spacious corridor running in parallel to the monumental, colonnaded front elevation. One side of this corridor showed extensive murals, illustrating the vast industrial output of the country.

A fourth gallery was dedicated to 'A Fitter Britain' demonstrating that the might of a nation lay in the health and wellbeing of its people as much as in its industrial muscle. This theme was symbolised in a powerful sculpture of a family group by Barney Seale. The Health and Fitness Hall demonstrated in graphic and concrete form a wide range of educational and recreational resources dedicated to the physical and mental wellbeing available to the citizens of the United Kingdom, from sport and a good wholesome food

supply to the eradication of slums. A giant mechanical man and other models, offered an insight into the physiology of the human body.

The exterior of the United Kingdom Pavilion was also suitably grand in scale and ornamentation. At one end of its linear fronting lake, two gilded lions guarded the wide stairway up to the main entrance. Tall windows were topped by three golden, figurative sculptures over which fluttered the Union Jack. In the Exit Hall, a steel and glass globe revolved as if unsupported in space. Externally the relatively modestly proportioned exit was flanked by a lake on either side. A large gilded relief of Britannia demonstrated Britain's continuing dominion over the waves.

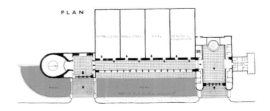

ABOVE. One of two imperial gilded lions guarding the entrance to the building. RIGHT. The detailed plan showing the ornamental pools in which the building was dramatically reflected.

THE GARDEN CLUB

Other than Tait's masterpiece, the Tower of Empire commanding the top of Bellahouston Hill, The Garden Club was probably the most prominently sited building in the entire Exhibition. The Garden Club, by Thomas Marwick, was brilliantly linked to the architectural delights below by a dramatically illuminated flight of stairs and a cascade cut into the hill. 'Study of Youth', a sculpture by Thomas Whalen, marked the end of the stairway.

The cleverly designed Club was a series of interlinked forms and experiences leading to a sumptuous interior – as would justify the pricey membership fees. A drum, or rotunda, on the western end of an open, curved colonnade, housed small shops while a series of interlocked forms at the other end accommodated the lounge, bar and restaurant. On the exterior was a wrap around, long, canopied tea terrace from which visitors, shielded from the sun and rain, could observe the Colonial and Dominion Avenue below or appreciate the longer view towards the Eaglesham Hills and the rural landscape to the south of the city.

LEFT. The dramatic sweep of the colonnade with canopied tea terrace beyond is captured in this view taken by the Exhibition's official photographer. ABOVE. A view looking northwards to the Garden Club with the Tower of Empire behind taken from the South Bandstand.

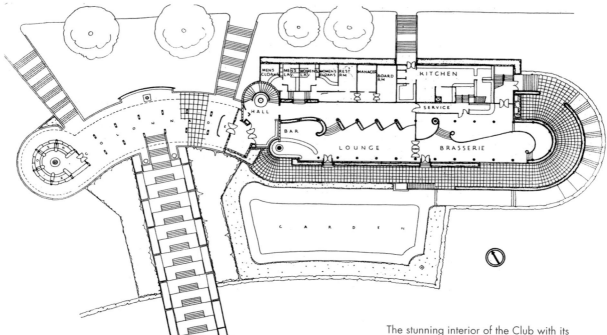

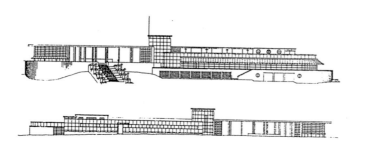

ABOVE. Detailed plan and elevations.

The stunning interior of the Club with its elongated, 'S' shaped, lighting arrangement and encircling row of pillars, formally echoed a free-flowing building plan. Comfortably fitted out with modern furniture and a glass bar attended by uniformed waiting staff, it could easily have been part of a great ocean liner as well as a tribute to Clydeside design and craft.

Two floors were linked by a curved staircase with water spraying from above into a pool at the bottom, the centre-piece of which was a stylised water-nymph sculpture by Norman Forest. In place of a handrail, the stairway was enclosed by an open fine-metal mesh structure, rising to the roof 50 feet above.

A sculpture on the outside of the building by Hugh Lorimer and Thomas Whalen's 'Mother and Child' on the roof provided further artistic embelishment.

Basil Spence's spectacular ICI Pavilion showing the three pylons 'Earth, Air and Water' with the rotunda behind. Spence introduced a series of symbols, treated in relief, on the three themes.

ICI PAVILION

Basil Spence, was one of the bright young turks selected by Thomas Tait to participate in his design team. In the year before the Empire Exhibition, Tait arranged for Spence to visit the 1937 Paris exhibition, 'Exposition Internationale des Arts et Techniques dans la Vie Moderne' where the 30 year old Spence, already established as Scotland's leading modernist architect, enjoyed the bold displays of modern European architectural thinking and the brightly contemporary artistic collaboration.

Spence's ICI Pavilion was the most distinctive and theatrical building of the entire Exhibition. Three tall pylons, two of which were utilised as entry points to a windowless drum-shaped enclosure were as close to sculpture as to architecture. The pylons were designed to represent Earth, Air and Water - the three elements which provide the raw materials for the chemical industry. These were depicted in repeated reliefs, by the ubiquitous Thomas Whalen, on each of the three concave faces which constituted each tower. The three structures were connected by narrow bands worked in non-ferrous metal. The fourth element, Fire, was symbolised by a beam of light projecting skyward through a coloured column of water located centrally between the pylons.

Spence worked closely with ICI and artists to provide an informative exhibition within the Pavilion which celebrated the company's international reputation while its use of materials and processes - such as the development of the new material, coloured perspex - were highlighted in carefully staged exhibits, including murals by Donald Moodie and Robert H Westwater. Empire shields were painted on the external walls of the rotunda by Walter Pritchard who also made the decorative metal frogs which lined the pool at the base of the pylons. The company's catalogue paid tribute to the fact that 'the design, construction and decoration have been entirely in the hands of Scotsmen'.

WOMEN OF THE EMPIRE PAVILION

Although this Pavilion occupied an important site opposite the United Kingdom Pavilion and was designed by a talented and determined woman, the official Exhibition Guide choose not to credit Margaret Brodie with its authorship. The Women of the Empire Pavilion, coloured in dove grey, blue and silver and complete with lily pond, was a serious, functional building which cleverly housed a number of activities.

Containing a reception room, three exhibition halls, a fashion theatre, a laboratory, tearoom and bureau of advice on dietetics, it demonstrated the involvement of women in the arts, crafts and industry in Britain and across the Empire. Interior decoration, painting and embroidery featured and fashion shows were staged four times each day in the 400-seat auditorium. A curved exhibition hall, around yet detached from the fashion theatre, displayed costumes from historic times to the present day.

Three halls displayed everything ranging from handicrafts and cosmetics to weaving and illuminated manuscripts. Located on a landing mid way between the second and third halls, a circular stained glass panel symbolised women. The third hall was dedicated to women's organisations and contained a twenty-four foot long mural depicting the various trades and professions in which women were engaged. The mural artist Sadie McLellan also designed the stained glass window.

A 'Children's Corner' displayed drawings by children from all over the Empire.

ABOVE LEFT. Margaret Brodie's Women of the Empire Pavilion seen from one of the pools that fronted the UK Pavilion. The Atlantic Restaurant dominates the hill behind. ABOVE. The Fashion Theatre.

TOWER OF EMPIRE

Tait's Tower, as it quickly became known, was an inescapable sight from any point in Bellahouston Park, catching the eye and the imagination of visitors. The structure, a very real 'tour de force', was a powerful demonstration of Glasgow's engineering skills and topped by a 36 foot high blue vane, like a rudder in the wind. Indeed, it was visible from many parts of the city and provided a startlingly modern view from the windows of Glasgow tenements. A backdrop to endless photographs of families, workers and school-children, it became the ultimate souvenir image, an icon. The Tower of Empire was Glasgow's Eiffel Tower, Empire State Building and Big Ben rolled into one.

Tait's master-plan for the Exhibition was designed around his 300 foot Tower. Set within a densely wooded area on top of the hill, it provided wide vistas to the Campsie Fells to the north, along the Clyde estuary westwards to the Highlands and Islands and a view of the shipyards, streets, houses and factories of Glasgow below. This was in stark contrast to the transient layout of the Exhibition itself - an artificial and temporary townscape of palaces and pavilions, wide avenues, neon lights, and strikingly modern architecture.

The magic of the Tower was not confined to its height and slender aerodynamic modernism. A smaller pavilion wrapped around the base not only allowed visitors access to the lifts and seemingly endless stairs, it also provided a dining experience with views at treetop level. A mandate from the Park's Department forbade the removal of mature trees so the Treetops Restaurant, built on stilts within the tree canopy, allowed living trees to be a significant and unusual feature of the interior.

Digital rendering of Thomas Tait's crowning achievement, the 300 foot high Tower of Empire.

PALACE OF ENGINEERING

The Exhibition's homage to engineering was its largest building with a frontage 465 feet long and a depth of 315 feet. The official guide to the Exhibition stressed the importance of engineers in the advancement of the Empire, linking the subject in romantic terms to the 'laying low' of jungles, draining swamps, building roads, railway bridges and dams. The guide also claimed that the building was equal in size to Buckingham Palace.

Within a six columned front facade, the main entrance of the Palace of Engineering occupied almost the full width in grand manner. While the building was simple and fairly austere, two large and colourful murals by C L Davidson were applied to the rounded wings on either side of the colonnade. These depicted the many and diverse forms of engineering with automobiles, bridges, dams, planes, ships and locomotives proclaiming the strength and dynamic modernism of British engineering. A restaurant and offices were contained within the rounded wings to either side of the front elevation. The Palace of Engineering was built by world renowned Glasgow structural steel firm Sir William Arrol & Co. in an astonishing 3 months.

Inside the industrial scale building – a huge hangar with exposed girders and a glazed roof – the exhibits were grouped uniformly in sections. Almost 240 stands covered everything from electricity and gas to marine engineering. A 'general' section explained the production of objects from sealing wax to shoes. A further section, organised by the Home Office, focused on safety in the factory and what was being done across the country to reduce the number of accidents in the workplace.

The detailed design of the Palace of Engineering was undertaken by Launcelot Ross elaborating upon Thomas Tait's initial plan and sketches.

The Palace of Engineering was the largest building in the Exhibition, testimony to British engineering expertise in 1938. The Palace was fronted by two very large murals depicting scenes from industry. Much of this building survives to this day as an aviation workshop at Prestwick Airport.

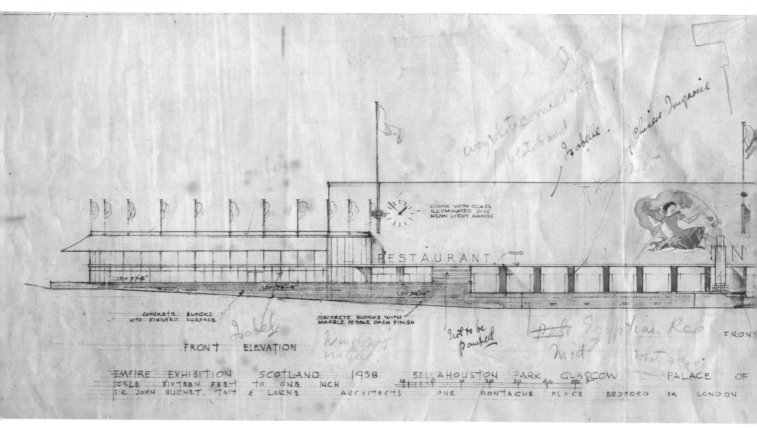

ABOVE. A fascinating drawing showing the front elevation of the Palace of Industry West complete with annotations and updates possibly by Tait himself. *Courtesy of Archives and Special Collections, Mitchell Library, Glasgow.* LEFT. This view of the facade with its simple but striking form helps to explain why the architecture of the Empire Exhibition looked so different in 1938. The mural illustration in the sketch above changed in the actual building.

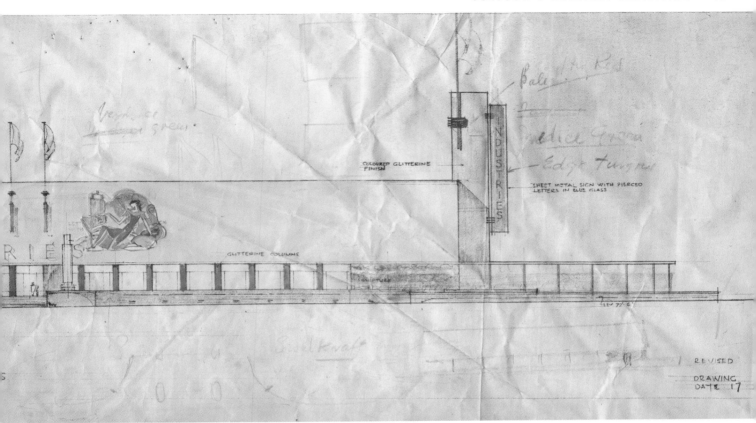

PALACE OF INDUSTRY WEST

The Palace of Industry West was the second largest of the Exhibition's structures, its scale exceeded only by the behemoth Palace of Engineering. Both sat, like mighty bookends, at the opposite ends of the Dominions and Colonies Avenue. Designed by J Taylor Thomson, its frontage, over 500 feet in length, was built in a broad inward curve, encompassing low windows recessed behind rounded piers on either side of the main entrance. Above, taking up around three quarters of the height of the front facade, was a large expanse of plain wall punctuated by two painted motifs by Charles Baillie, 'Man

Harnessing the Elements' and a similarly idealised but female figure, 'Released Energy'. The murals add an interesting graphic dynamic to an otherwise plain frontage.

A restaurant and terrace were located at the south end of the pavilion's main elevation, disrupting the symmetry of the composition. In anticipation of visitors' healthy appetites, a further buffet restaurant with its own terrace was placed at the opposite end. The building was formed in the manner of a factory, three wings projecting back like a splayed letter 'E' in plan. The roofs of the wings were extensively glazed to capitalise on natural light.

The demand for space to display Britain's industry necessitated the creation of a second Palace of Industry. The two Pavilions were distinct from each other in content. The latter, known as the Palace of Industry North, was largely concerned with furniture and textiles while West promoted food and beverages (almost half of the area taken up by the Cooperative Wholesale Society).

A view of the Palace of Industry North from Kingsway looking towards the Tower of Empire which is just visible in the distance.

PALACE OF INDUSTRY NORTH

Designed by Jack Coia from sketches by Tait, the Palace of Industry North was situated between the Canadian and Burmese Pavilions. The entrance, modest in scale was from an open courtyard screened by a decorative glass wall. Within a timbered hallway, a mural by Hugh Adam Crawford, provided a backdrop to furniture exhibits. Like most buildings in the Exhibition, Industry North was constructed almost entirely in wood faced with white painted asbestos sheeting. A long row of white painted windows running in a frieze at roof height provided natural light.

The Main Hall exhibited products such as furniture, glassware and pottery. Stands were designed as open displays allowing sight lines to extend along the length of the building. Two smaller halls presented world famous Scottish textiles while decorative murals illustrated their use. Unusually in the Exhibition, detached external showcases lined the main facade, designed to tempt visitors into the Pavilion. The impressive staircase was exposed in a short illuminated tower, rounded and glazed on one end. The tower and entrance porch were painted a rich terracotta red.

Diagonally opposite the main entrance to the pavilion, Coia cleverly designed a small exhibition area at the rear of the building, This contained photographic murals displaying Post Office systems.

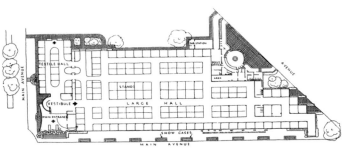

PLAN

THE SCOTTISH PAVILIONS

Twin Scottish pavilions designed by Basil Spence, each a mirror image of the other, commanded attention at the Paisley Road West entrance. Distinctive in colour and form, with the tower and vane motif much favoured by Thomas Tait, these were in stark contrast to the dark, brooding tenements on the other side of the perimeter fence.

Together these pavilions told Scotland's story. The Scottish Pavilion North was dedicated to planning and the services available within modern Scottish communities. Opposite the Scottish Pavilion South dramatically portrayed Scottish history. The past was also portrayed by the nearby 'An Clachan', a popular stage-set version of a Highland village with renderings of 'real' highland dwellings by the academic architect Dr Colin Sinclair.

ABOVE. The 25 foot statue of St Andrew by Archibald Dawson located in Scottish Pavilion South in front of a saltire. RIGHT. Both Scottish Pavilions seen from the Tower of Empire in their proper context opposite one another on the Scottish Avenue.

THE SCOTTISH PAVILION NORTH consisted of three areas; a large Entrance Hall, the Hall of Health and Planning and the Hall of Education. The lofty Entrance Hall with its large bowed window contained a twenty-five foot high sculpture by Thomas Whalen. 'Service' depicted a seated figure holding the Staff of Health in her left hand and the Torch of Knowledge in her right.

In the Hall of Health a large mural painted by Walter Pritchard, symbolised the content of the display. In addition to models, diagrams and photo-murals covering pre-natal care to old age, a three-dimensional map of Scotland, 5 feet below floor level and covering 500 square feet, indicated the main natural and civil engineering features of the country.

The Hall of Education showed arts and crafts produced by children between starting and leaving school. In the entrance hall, exhibits illustrated Scotland's rich cultural and literary output since the end of the Great War. On the outside of the building, on terra-cotta coloured blocks, stood sculptures depicting Burns, Carlyle, Livingstone, Scott and Watt.

A digital nightime view of Scottish Pavilion South seen over the top of the Royal Fountain on Scottish Avenue.

THE SCOTTISH PAVILION SOUTH was similarly sub-divided into 3 sections. The Entrance Hall gave the impression of having been constructed from great blocks of masonry. As in North, a huge sculpture was placed to confront visitors. This 25 foot high figure of St Andrew with arms outstretched standing in the prow of a symbolic boat, stood in front of a floor-to-ceiling bowed window. The sculptor Archibald Dawson was the Head of Sculpture at Glasgow School of Art. Sadly, just after completing this extraordinary work, the largest of his career, Dawson collapsed and died. His St Andrew, like most of the Empire Exhibition's sculptural works, did not endure beyond the term of the Exhibition. Fortunately many other works, cast in bronze, are an enduring memorial to Dawson's considerable talent.

A massive St Andrew's Cross with the image of the Saint within it, was sandblasted into the glass, a significant statement from the outside. Two large tapestries, woven by the Marquis of Bute's Edinburgh company, hung in the hall.

A Hall of History chronicled the rise of Scotland from prehistorythrough the Roman occupation up to the time of the Covenanters using illuminated manuscripts and Paisley shawls. The final section, the Hall of Youth, making a natural link to the Scottish Pavilion North, was devoted to modern social services and highlighted clubs for boys and girls using photo-murals. Club rooms were provided for meetings throughout the Exhibition. A sculpture by Andrew Dods symbolised youth while a striking mural by William Semple promoted the organisations concerned with care of the young.

The Beresford Hotel - designed by W Beresford Inglis in 1938 to accommodate visitors to the Empire Exhibition. The original colours were bright yellow faience tiles and bright red fins.

4 I WAS THERE...
ARCHITECTS AND INFLUENCES
DAVID J LESLIE, ARCHITECT

It is a comment on my seniority that I am able to claim, with some pride, that I was there - at Bellahouston Park for the Empire Exhibition of 1938. I admit that my recollections of the Exhibition are almost negligible – I was just a child being taken around by my mother in uncomfortably wet circumstances. I was certainly not aware of the Exhibition's stunning display of architectural modernism. It would be a romantic notion to attribute the 'off the wall' decision of my mid teens to become an architect, to the influence of the Exhibition. That would be to stretch the imagination beyond reality.

It is however a fascinating study, as an architect, to ponder the impact of this Exhibition on the Glasgow and wider community of 1938. On face value, it was an incredible display of the power and resources of the Empire – or as King George VI intoned, 'the Commonwealth of Nations'. I am tempted to ask myself, was the Exhibition a very public warning to Mr Hitler, in a time of political tension, not to meddle with us!

Certainly there were militaristic references within the murals on the Palace of Engineering and on the carousel in the Amusement Park suggesting that such topics were in the minds of the creators. There was also an Army and Air Force Pavilion. The inscription stones sent from institutions around the Commonwealth to be built into the Peace Monument serve as a poignant reminder of the war clouds gathering in 1938.

In this electronic age of modern convenience, it is difficult to appreciate the impact the Empire Exhibition must have made. Indeed, one of the few memories I have of the event is the pride in which my parents held the achievement - appreciative customers in their day with several repeat visits. To understand the impression the Exhibition made on people at that time we should remind ourselves of the conditions of the day.

Glasgow was a large bustling city whose architecturally outstanding buildings were hardly appreciated, covered as they were with the black soot of industry and commerce. My grandparents, in common with the majority of city dwellers, lived in a 'black' tenement with no electric light and no bath. A cheery coal fire, set in a polished and gleaming black-leaded kitchen range, was the centre piece of family life around which home entertainment occurred. Bathing was in a galvanised tub in front of the fire with water warmed in a black kettle heated on the kitchen range.

Into this large industrial city scene was injected a small town of modern buildings, many of outstanding architectural quality, floodlit at night, landscaped between pools of glittering water with jetted fountains illuminated in vivid colour. A wonder-world indeed of sheer escapism for the community – but a wonder world soon to be erased from memory by the horrors of war. The author of this marvel was architect-in-chief Thomas Smith Tait who gathered a team of architects together to execute his vision for the Empire Exhibition. These architects either had a direct connection with Tait through the John Burnet practice or had caught his eye in practice with the application of the modern style.

Thus Margaret Brodie, A D Bryce, Jack Coia, A Esme Gordon, Thomas Waller Marwick, Launcelot Ross, Gordon Tait, James Taylor Thomson and Basil Spence were brought together. Reports indicate that these architects took part with Tait in the development of the Exhibition masterplan and one can easily

Le Chateau, Silver End - one of a group of houses designed by Thomas Tait in 1927 for the steel window manufacturer W F Crittal, represents the first 'cubist' design houses in Britain. *Courtesy of RIBA Library Photographs Collection.*

imagine that individuals of such architectural stature must have contributed to the overall concept by a free exchange of ideas. Each would later carry out an executive function in the creation of individual buildings.

Attribution of building design is frequently difficult in architectural practices or in team efforts such as the design of the Empire Exhibition. The question arises 'What is the contribution of the master and what of the assistant?' Indeed architectural literature has varied in attribution of design of buildings in the Exhibition.

Reviewing the buildings it is clear that a common architectural modernism pervades and is likely to have been promoted by Thomas Tait, as lead architect with the team of architects he appointed followed that style closely. This seems to be confirmed by the fact that drawings still exist which show that in the case of the Palace of Industries and the Garden Club, for example, Burnet Tait & Lorne did prepare design drawings. It is indicative of the strength of the design control that the quality of modern design remained consistent throughout virtually the entire exhibition. The sketch designs of the major pavilions were superbly expressed by the executive architects.

As an architect, I ask myself what impact did the Exhibition have on post war architectural design? The Second World War created a schism in the development of architectural style, when almost no major buildings were undertaken. Architects returning from the war – like everybody coming back from the services – were looking for

Hawkhead Infectious Diseases Hospital, Paisley – designed by Thomas Tait in 1935 and selected as the first premiated scheme in an architectural competition. *Courtesy RIAS Collection/Swan.*

the 'brave new world', shaking off the dust and grime of the past. Renewal after urban decay, modernism and functionalism became the theme.

Launcelot Ross and James Thomson established major Glasgow firms – Launcelot Ross & Lindsay and Thomson McCrea and Saunders. Margaret Brodie took up full time teaching at Glasgow School of Architecture where she was a major influence on many students who passed through her hands, instilling in them a strong commitment to functionalism.

Of all the architects who took part in the exhibition, Basil Spence and Jack Coia went on to make the greatest impact on post war architecture. Spence had a spectacular career, honoured for his service to architecture,

establishing himself as a leading designer of exhibitions during
the Festival of Britain in 1951, winning the Coventry Cathedral
competition and designing many projects across the country including
Glasgow Airport at Abbotsinch, the now demolished Queen Elizabeth
Flats in Gorbals, Hyde Park Cavalry Barracks and the British Embassy
in Rome.

Jack Coia re-established the practice of Gillespie Kidd and Coia as
leading exponents of church design, taking Andy MacMillan and Isi
Metzstein into partnership. By the mid fifties, MacMillan and Metzstein
were responsible for many new churches and University projects
which brought Coia the Royal Gold Medal in 1969.

An influence continuing through the war years into post-war
Britain however was the adoption of the 'flat roof' of the Thirties,
with the legacy of problems that was to bring. Its
most obvious influence in a local Glasgow sense is
represented by the move from the Scottishness of the
garden suburbs of Mosspark designed by Chief Housing
Architect , Robert Horne, (1920 – 23) and Knightswood
(1923 – 31) to the cubist styled development of flat
roofed houses in Penilee designed by Chief Housing
Architect J H Ferrie between 1939 and 1947. The
Penilee houses nevertheless did not persist with the
'whiteness' associated with the Exhibition, greys and
browns being preferred.

Nor did the authorities pay much attention to the
prototype houses built for the Empire Exhibition commissioned by the
Scottish Council for Art and Industry, a country house by Basil Spence
and working class flats by Mervyn Noad. The latter was dismissed by
the Director of Housing as too expensive, having no direct access to
the front and a number of other minor details which 'offended' him.

Studying architecture during the Fifties my attention was not drawn
to the modernism of the Empire Exhibition – though I did admire it.
The increasing impact of the printed media on my young professional
career turned attention directly to the leaders of the modern movement

Rosshill Avenue, Penilee, designed by J H Ferrie,
Glasgow's Chief Housing Architect and built between
1939 and 1947 - probably the first flat-roofed
public housing in Glasgow. *Courtesy Archives and
Special Collections, Mitchell Library, Glasgow.*

TOP. The Luma Factory is a good example of a tasteful conversion into housing by Cornelius McClymont Architects showing sympathetic alterations to the original façade. *Courtesy Archives and Special Collections, Mitchell Library, Glasgow.* ABOVE. The Luma Factory, designed by SCWS architect Cornelius Armour in 1936 for the manufacture of electric light bulbs with a dramatic tower representing the building's purpose.

– Le Corbusier, Walter Gropius, Mies van der Rohe, Marcel Breuer and other stalwarts who were pushing out the boundaries of modernism – like Basil Spence himself. Functionalism was important to me – the function of the building expressed in its architecture and derived from its plan. We rejoiced in the possibilities of new building technologies – steel frames to behold and not covered by architectural ornament, and concrete, 'off the shutter'.

For the man in the street, the years following the Second World War brought austerity and political change resulting from the nation's near bankruptcy. There was a period when the economic climate and the largest of all programmes of urban renewal, during the fifties and sixties, was to drive down building cost standards. Cost standards for public architecture did not adequately provide for pitched roofs more suited to the Scottish climate. The scale of renewal also could have been said to affect architectural style, when the modernism was freed from constraints of having to sit comfortably with older architectural styles. Added to this, changes in building legislation, standardisation, prefabrication, development of structural grids to accommodate car parking have all exercised their influence of the architectural character of the fifties, sixties and seventies.

Many mistakes were made during this period of urban renewal when the fabric of cities was torn apart to create an illusory new Utopia, without taking care to ensure that the lives of the people living in cities were not also torn apart. Glasgow for example moved from being a matriarchal society, where 'mother' lived around the corner to help support the young mums and families, to a society where these links were severed by distance – by migration to new districts or new towns. Insufficient infrastructure and management was allowed for the new high-rise living, coupled with construction methods with poor standards of insulation.   It took almost three decades before lessons were learned, and more attention given to an architectural heritage which frequently conflicted with new building standards.

It is difficult therefore to identify clear influences of architectural style of the Empire Exhibition on post war architecture, but looking back on it now, there can be no denying the outstanding quality of architectural design of the Exhibition, and indeed, the detail which the presenters of the exhibition managed to impart in their exhibits.

The Empire Exhibition was an event of quite extraordinary design quality, demonstrating the virility of the 'Commonwealth of Nations'. The sheer quantity of art work on display, the graphic design, the quality and content of exhibition displays are something to wonder at even today. Listening to the interviews of those 'who were there', during the research stages of this project, 'awe and wonder' comes over loud and clear – the bright and attractive colours on buildings, the power of the water displays, the 'fairyland' illuminations – all features which spirited people away from the dullness of their surroundings.

There can be no doubting the vivid images which Glasgow's greatest exhibition imprinted in memory. There are significant lessons to be learned from further study of its design and delivery which would undoubtedly serve us well today.

St Andrews House, Edinburgh. Thomas Tait's most prestigious commission in Scotland was built in 1933 and probably led to his appointment as architect for the Empire Exhibition. *Courtesy of RIAS and RCAHMS.*

5 3D MODEL DEVELOPMENT
DOUGLAS PRITCHARD, HEAD OF VISUALISATION
THE DIGITAL DESIGN STUDIO, GLASGOW SCHOOL OF ART

A work in progress wireframe rendering of the Garden Club and Tower of Empire. The image does not include textures but indicates the level of 3D modelling and light levels.

SITE

The contours of the terrain at Bellahouston Park and the placement of all the Exhibition buildings were based on the developed pre-1938 site plan submitted by a member of the public. Through our research, it was identified that while some of the buildings were not indicated on this plan, the location of existing vegetation as well as the contours of the site were. Bellahouston Park is dominated by a hill which thus became a significant landscape feature of the Exhibition.

This large-scale drawing was digitally scanned and imported into 2D CAD software. The drawing's contour lines, roads and pathways were traced using series of splines and this was then exported into the 3D software from which the terrain was derived. The placement of the trees was based on the original site drawing, with smaller scale vegetation located from the aerial and other photographs.

ENVIRONMENT

The lighting of the model was based on the Daylight system within 3D Studio Max. This allows for a geo-specific lighting that corresponds to the time and date required for the renderings or animations. All of the project lighting is based on 15 July 1938 under a cloud free sky.   Given the actual conditions of the event, often heavy rain, the software also allows for exceptionally cloudy or rainy lighting conditions.

ARCHITECTURE

Of the entire Exhibition only one building, The Palace of Art, is currently in existence. This building was photographed and physically measured to derive its 3D representation. Although, as noted, there was a lack of architectural drawings to generate the 3D buildings, there was an abundance of original photographs collected in advance and during the modelling. In total there were over 230 colour and back and white paper photographs. All of this information was digitally scanned and filed according to each venue. All but three buildings had clear imagery of the front and entry facades. The less photogenic rear facades or service entrances were not well documented. Occasionally these facades would be picked up incidentally but the majority of detailing for these areas was based on advice from the Panel.

A view of the untextured 3D model of the Tower of Empire and South Cascade and Grand Staircase.

A view of the Atlantic Restaurant and the south-side of the exhibition. The fully textured rendering is on the front cover.

Because of the irregular collection of images and experience in the development of the 3D Virtual City of Glasgow project which the modelling team were working on concurrently with the Empire project, it was determined that single image photogrammetry was not an appropriate solution for this particular project. The layout and proportions were based on ortho-rectification in a combination of Adobe Photoshop and Autocad.

Heights and dimensions of buildings that originated from photographs were based on a variety of visual cues. Standardised panel systems, which were extensively used in the original Exhibition construction as well as entryway steps, provided the modellers with guidance. Unfortunately, the virtual representation of a number of buildings had to be based on dimensions derived from people standing in front of the structures.